# THE TAO OF
# BUSINESS
# WITTICISMS

BY

PIETER KLAAS JAGERSMA

*Dedicated to business people
around the globe.*

# CONTENTS

# 1 PREFACE

THE TAO OF Business Witticisms provides 500 insights, tricks of the trade, maxims, humorous truths, and anecdotal phrases on organizations, managers, and the habits of leaders and their followers. It brings together wisdom about what works and doesn't work in companies and organizations.

Some witticisms may seem trivial, but each and everyone of them has the potential to trigger you into action. The book is based on experience and written with the practicing executive, manager, and entrepreneur in mind, mixing insights with a good laugh. The Tao of Business Witticisms is informative and encouraging.

The axioms and provocative perspectives on management, leadership, and business represent a more or less selective debriefing of my work as an entrepreneur, supervisory board member, and professor. The axioms presented have proved invaluable to me as a professional.

I reasoned that if the most useful, entertaining, and funniest of them were collected, put between a front and back cover, and published, I would have an interesting manual for creative thinking. Hopefully they show how essential things can be phrased in a short, simple, and quotable form combining truth, humor, and common sense. As always, they need context. After all, it's the message that counts.

Writing equals fun. But as always, it is a long-term, time-consuming activity. While you must serve your readers first, you need to reserve some of your 'prime time' for self-development if you're going to serve them better tomorrow than you serve them today. Thanks, Yvette, for most of this development!

In making this book, I would like to express special thanks to all the senior and junior business people, politicians as well as professional friends for their 'contributions'. I got a lot of mileage out of making this book.

I wish all of you a pleasant odyssey and hope that my experience as a messenger of helpful axioms and opinions shows through. I hope they make sense in your context. If you have any thoughts or comments you'd like to share, I'd be delighted to hear from you. Address all correspondence to me at: pkj@wxs.nl.

Let's keep the conversation and dialogue going!

Pieter Klaas Jagersma,
Summer 2014

## 2 BUSINESS WITTICISMS

---

### 1

*Never make snowballs for the boss to throw at proposals – the outcome could be an avalanche.*

---

### 2

*Although your clients vary in size, the size of your commitment shouldn't.*

---

### 3

*Consultant: a child of the last recession.*

---

### 4

*The assumed price should always seem higher than the actual price.*

## 5

*Your people are your product.*

## 6

*Vision is a light that seduces the soul.*

## 7

*Be inspired by the past, but built for the future.*

## 8

*Although business is all about cash flow,*
*'cash' is less important than 'flow'.*

## 9

*Your strategy for the future is to make sure there is a future.*

## 10

*Your challenge is the human condition.*

## 11

*Great entrepreneur: rebel without a pause.*

## 12

*While many organizations announce 'strategic alliances', many lack 'alliance strategies'.*

## 13

*Techniques only produce a temporary advantage.*

## 14

*You cannot shrink to excellence.*

## 15

*A 'big' reputation is like a 'small' poem.*

## 16

*Never confuse activity with results.*

## 17

*The relationship is the job.*

## 18

*Be superlative, never comparative.*

## 19

*Nobody owes you a job.*

## 20

*Organizations are slower than people in changing behavior.*

## 21

*It is the price, not the product,*
*that is sold to the customer.*

## 22

*Nothing is more dangerous than a strategy*
*when it's the only one you have.*

## 23

*Give clients what they need, not what they ask.*

## 24

*Average is one step from below average.*

## 25

*Money talks but doesn't think.*

## 26

*Big mistakes are OK as long as they are fixed by the right people.*

## 27

*Top performers are more like comets than stars.*

## 28

*Ideas must be dangerous.*

## 29

*If you've reached the top, don't
forget to enjoy the view.*

## 30

*Fame can be bought but reputation
has to be earned.*

## 31

*Train yourself to look for the surprise.*

## 32

*When things go wrong, retreat temporarily.*

## 33

*Leaders don't sit only at the top of pyramids.*

## 34

*Talented people need organizations less than organizations need talented people.*

## 35

*Character is all about retaining a strong identity.*

## 36

*Ideas are worthless unless they are shared.*

## 37

*Visualize the message, not the mess.*

## 38

*Risk is what you make of it.*

## 39

*Client: walking data generator.*

## 40

*Reverse your viewpoint regularly.*

## 41

*Never allow voting.*

## 42

*The client is the giant.*

## 43

*Follow the bouncing ball.*

## 44

*Be disciplined about removing details.*

## 45

*The senior manager is always the last to know.*

## 46

*Just because you can, doesn't mean you should.*

## 47

*Consider equipment and facilities your worst enemies and treat them as your best friends.*

## 48

*Good practices are always best practices.*

## 49

*Pass on values, not assets.*

## 50

*You sell to someone before you sell something.*

## 51

*Revolutions in markets are always preceded*

*by revolutions in measurement.*

## 52

*Go internal before you go external.*

**53**

*Manufacture fame, but don't forget
to convert it into fortune.*

**54**

*Say it with pictures.*

**55**

*The promise of value is the key to
differentiation, not an alternative to it.*

**56**

*Make strength productive and weakness irrelevant.*

## 57

*Brilliance is a matter of timing.*

## 58

*Bankruptcy: portal of discovery.*

## 59

*The best insights don't condense neatly into bullet points.*

## 60

*Never fail at failure.*

## 61

*Risks cannot please everyone.*

## 62

*Everything matters!*

## 63

*Communicate, don't advertise.*

## 64

*Select customers — don't let them select you.*

## 65

*Starting an organization with a great idea might be a bad idea.*

## 66

*Judgment: leading signal in the noise.*

## 67

*The best companies are repositories of skills that are hard to replicate.*

## 68

*Out of friction comes insight.*

## 69

*Information is the single greatest change agent in history.*

## 70

*Never act as a messenger, even if it means that you hear fewer messages.*

## 71

*Make a mistake seem easy to correct.*

## 72

*Most advantages are not self-sustainable, but, self-destructive.*

## 73

*Creativity is most valuable when it is more difficult to achieve.*

## 74

*In a competitive context, the better an idea, the shorter its life.*

## 75

*When you speak, control the volume.*

## 76

*The absence of competition is not the same as collaboration.*

## 77

*Businesses are about creating change for other businesses.*

## 78

*Find people who are at ease being part of something.*

## 79

*If it can't be simplified, it doesn't belong on the screen.*

## 80

*Control your expenses better than your competitors.*

---

## 81

*Leadership requires not giving direction, but taking it.*

---

## 82

*If you want to fly, don't clip your wings!*

---

## 83

*To see the forest, you must identify each tree.*

---

## 84

*Return is just a measure.*

## 85

*Give yourself the benefit of the time you can afford.*

## 86

*Progress is a well-known language*
*that nobody understands.*

## 87

*You achieve what you prepare for.*

## 88

*Make sure the esprit is about the right corps.*

## 89

*A single number to indicate the health of anything*

*is a poor representation of a multi-layered reality.*

## 90

*Win access to the ear.*

## 91

*Everybody is a market.*

## 92

*Historic achievements begin every morning.*

## 93

*Put opportunity ahead of security.*

## 94

*Characters rarely age well.*

## 95

*Experience matters less than your ability to learn.*

## 96

*Accept inequalities if they are coupled
with equality of opportunities.*

## 97

*Put a little weekend in your week.*

## 98

*You can only get real recognition abroad.*

## 99

*Quality cannot be measured – that's quantity.*

## 100

*Employees learn the most when teaching others.*

---

## 101

*Excellent firms are the best places to fail.*

---

## 102

*Do you get what you do, or do you*
*do what you have to do?*

---

## 103

*You cannot save yourself rich.*

---

## 104

*In two days, the future will be the past.*

## 105

*Opportunity comes often.*

## 106

*Executives must understand the difference
between being interesting to their employees
and being interested in them.*

## 107

*A leader must attract attention.*

## 108

*Failure no. 1 – talking when you don't know
what you're talking about. So don't.*

## 109

*An organization cannot be brought to the summit while maintaining harmony.*

## 110

*High-principle businesses attract high-caliber people.*

## 111

*The more opportunities to hand off the ball, the greater the likelihood of a fumble.*

## 112

*Leaders deal in forests that subordinates create from many individual trees.*

## 113

*Be a maestro at mental leaps.*

## 114

*You can outwork anyone.*

## 115

*Attention is the next business frontier.*

## 116

*Ear: most important body part*

*of a person in power.*

## 117

*Sometimes you need to go slow to go fast.*

## 118

*In business 'cool' needs to meet 'calm'.*

## 119

*Competition is as certain as death
but as complicated as hell.*

## 120

*Mental attitude beats mental
capacity seven days a week.*

## 121

*Success is a virtual reality.*

## 122

*It's all about growth without getting fat.*

## 123

*It is more important to learn what not to do than what to do.*

## 124

*A shift in direction by a market is more important than a move by a competitor.*

---

## 125

*People need direction, not management.*

---

## 126

*Magic comes by careful planning.*

---

## 127

*Exploit the benefit of not knowing
what you cannot achieve.*

---

## 128

*What you see depends on where you sit.*

## 129

*Entrepreneurship is an exercise in mythmaking.*

## 130

*A good idea is good, but never good enough.*

## 131

*Just put one foot in front of the other.*

## 132

*Executive truths become executive traps.*

## 133

*Question no. 1: can a person do the job?*

## 134

*Before you try to convince anyone else,
make sure that you are convinced.*

## 135

*Good gets better – bad gets worse.*

## 136

*People are not your most important
asset - the right people are.*

# 137

*Success is about cooperating to learn and learning to cooperate.*

# 138

*Create a place where you can be!*

# 139

*You cannot buy other people's opinions.*

# 140

*Leadership is neither simple nor sophisticated; it's either good or not.*

---

## 141

*Corruption is a symbol of relative decline.*

---

## 142

*Swim with the big fish.*

---

## 143

*You never get something for nothing.*

---

## 144

*Get everywhere because you're everywhere.*

## 145

*Understand and be understood.*

## 146

*Vision: gateway to the future.*

## 147

*Don't differentiate without a difference.*

## 148

*Persistence trumps talent.*

## 149

*Size matters but shape matters even more.*

## 150

*Imagination is your most important asset.*

## 151

*You will need more than eight hours a day to score the winning touchdown.*

## 152

*Missing a good opportunity is not as important as avoiding a bad one.*

## 153

*The analytically correct answer is not always the best answer.*

## 154

*A great idea is one which comes unbidden.*

## 155

*Start early.*

## 156

*Diversification = diworseification.*

## 157

*Fame is easier than fortune.*

## 158

*Be good at getting better.*

## 159

*You don't need to be a low-cost producer,
as long as you are the low-price provider
to the most profitable accounts.*

## 160

*The ultimate inspiration is in the deadline.*

## 161

*The way to business heaven: restricted choice.*

## 162

*Executives read reports to find out what they don't know; they don't read reports to find out what they already know.*

## 163

*You get what you negotiate.*

## 164

*Tell anyone anything without telling everyone everything.*

## 165

*Attention is a matter of judgment.*

## 166

*Be able to act sooner.*

## 167

*If you want to go in one direction, the best route often involves going in the other.*

## 168

*Success = SUM (will, skill, thrill)*

## 169

*Collaboration is the software of the future;*
*alliances are the hardware of the future.*

## 170

*The more valuable the talent, the*
*more difficult it is to manage.*

## 171

*Trust in business means different*
*things to different people.*

## 172

*Play is what you should do for a living – the*
*rest is organizing the results of the play.*

## 173

*Most things that you do not need to do
today are not worth doing at all.*

## 174

*Success comes in direct proportion to the
willingness to accept differences.*

## 175

*Don't win arguments that you ought to lose.*

## 176

*You have to know it before you grow it.*

## 177

*Put trust in the front room but keep skepticism in the back room.*

## 178

*Like good surgeons, the best employees are the busiest, and the busiest are often the best.*

## 179

*Gaining clarity does not necessarily eliminate uncertainty.*

## 180

*Never ruin the present by worrying over the future.*

## 181

*Reputation is not what you say it is; it's what they say it is.*

## 182

*The secret of fun is not in doing what one likes, but in liking what one does.*

## 183

*Look for clients, not business.*

## 184

*Satisfaction: 'killer virus' number one.*

## 185

*A dangerous business plan makes people think.*

## 186

*Margin: result of information asymmetry.*

## 187

*Specialist: generalist who knows something.*

## 188

*Shift the debate from whether an organization can achieve objectives to how it will achieve success.*

## 189

*There is no substitute for seeing for yourself.*

## 190

*Individualists belong in the boxing arena, not in organizations.*

## 191

*Develop new ideals, not just new ideas.*

## 192

*Change occurs when the change is easy to achieve.*

## 193

*Managers are answerable to one boss: the bottom line.*

## 194

*If you act in your clients' interest, it will ultimately also be in your best interest.*

## 195

*Great feelings cannot be described, they have to be experienced.*

## 196

*Integrity can't be bought.*

## 197

*Do you really need fun while driving?*

## 198

*The future is unevenly distributed.*

## 199

*Most problems call for common sense,*

*not management consultants.*

## 200

*Style should never get in the way of the story.*

## 201

*Penetrate with ideas, consolidate with methods, and conquer with imagination.*

## 202

*A great decision is threatened by ..... better decisions.*

## 203

*Success is all about the decisions you are allowed to make.*

## 204

*Manager: bureaucrat on the move.*

## 205

*Insights die if not aired in conversation.*

## 206

*Performance is the price of admission in a market.*

## 207

*Too many organizations are fighting
the weight of their own culture.*

## 208

*Avoid hot companies in hot countries.*

## 209

*Ally small first.*

## 210

*Calling a group a team doesn't make it one.*

## 211

*When things get bad, number 1 will catch a cold, number 2 will get pneumonia, and number 3 will disappear.*

## 212

*It's hard to tell whether a new idea is 'smart stupid' or 'stupid stupid'.*

## 213

*Education does not confer intelligence.*

## 214

*51 percent of nothing is still nothing.*

## 215

*Being successful involves doing a few things right and avoiding serious mistakes.*

## 216

*Identities advance reputation.*

## 217

*Exceptional improvements always start with ordinary employees.*

## 218

*It is harder to get a good idea accepted than to get a good idea.*

## 219

*Prestige is not without pain.*

## 220

*As long as there are risks there will be losses; when there are no risks, there will be no profits.*

## 221

*Experience and expertise are good;
brains and bravery are better.*

## 222

*Each affair has legs.*

## 223

*Never make judgments based on ratings.*

## 224

*Beliefs come before goals.*

## 225

*Every rule can be challenged; every dogma should be challenged.*

## 226

*If you cannot invent it, reinvent it.*

## 227

*Leaders are caught between their debt to the past and their commitment to the future.*

## 228

*Risk makes money.*

## 229

*The name of the game in business is not beating the competition but meeting customer needs.*

## 230

*Most companies perform far better today than they prepare for the future. That's why so many fail.*

## 231

*Executive education is good, executive development is better.*

## 232

*A business principle becomes stronger when you narrow the focus.*

## 233

*Unhappy customers are your greatest opportunity.*

## 234

*Be as offensive as possible, only*

*as defensive as necessary.*

## 235

*Play by the rules but don't think by the rules.*

## 236

*Wave laurels – don't rest on them.*

## 237

*Base your judgment on facts and prospects, not on a company's resume or a leader's speaking ability.*

## 238

*Good business ideas flow, great business ideas erupt.*

## 239

*Great strategies are long on detail and short on aspiration.*

## 240

*Employees must be willing to stand on each other's shoulders rather than on each other's toes.*

## 241

*Isolation isn't a bad thing if you believe you are in paradise.*

## 242

*Great executives live for tomorrow's race, not to analyze yesterday's performance.*

## 243

*Good R&D beats good marketing most days of the week.*

## 244

*The best innovation is imitation.*

## 245

*Business models need fixing, even
if they are not broken.*

## 246

*The first step toward greatness
is striving to achieve it.*

## 247

*Nothing exceeds like excess.*

## 248

*In a merger it takes ten pounds of energy
to produce one ounce of understanding.*

## 249

*If you don't talk that way, don't write that way!*

## 250

*Your identity is your destiny.*

## 251

*When you're caught in turbulence, instinct is all you've got to guide you through.*

## 252

*There's no such thing as a level playing field.*

## 253

*It's all about shaping the game you play,*
*not playing the game you find.*

## 254

*The road not taken can be very expensive.*

## 255

*Fear is the best virus of all.*

## 256

*You don't become less competitive*
*because competitors invest more.*

## 257

*Achieving success is less about overcoming challenges than about mastering things.*

## 258

*There is no end to the game of changing the game.*

## 259

*Excitement is the real project.*

## 260

*Customers don't care what you know until they know that you care.*

## 261

*Say "we" – as often as possible.*

## 262

*The best of deals are made at the worst of times – and vice versa.*

## 263

*Quality only matters when quantity is an inadequate substitute.*

## 264

*Prices in good times are often set by the companies that have the highest cost. Prices in bad times are always set by companies with the lowest cost.*

## 265

*Great firms are more interested in your
achievements than your particular area of expertise.*

## 266

*Competitors represent the past,
customers the future.*

## 267

*Manage things but lead people.*

## 268

*Great deals are built on cooperation,
not legal safeguards.*

## 269

*Promise only what you can deliver,*
*and deliver what you promise.*

## 270

*Competitive races are races to learn.*

## 271

*High expectations are a common*
*source of problems.*

## 272

*The most difficult culture to know is your own.*

## 273

*Always look for compatibility, but only after you have decided what sort of compatibility to seek.*

## 274

*Alliances don't work for you –*
*you work through them.*

## 275

*Successful merger or acquisition:*
*mission impossible.*

## 276

*Great initiatives are better than bad initiatives;*
*bad initiatives are better than no initiatives at all.*

## 277

*Organizations need promise-centric rather than product-centric business models.*

## 278

*The essence of entrepreneurship: timing.*

## 279

*Be misunderstood – occasionally.*

## 280

*Advice: bait for more advice.*

## 281

*Ask not what you can achieve but
what you can contribute.*

## 282

*Strategic plan: cryptogram.*

## 283

*All the evidence is on the field.*

## 284

*Great challenges = enormous problems.*

## 285

*Interesting suggestions are always expensive.*

## 286

*Great firms have more opportunities
than they have people.*

## 287

*Coaching is only available when you ask.*

## 288

*Invest at least as much time in building
a new strategy as you would in choosing
a new flatscreen television.*

## 289

*Find out everything essential by yourself.*

## 290

*Creativity has to be destructive to be constructive.*

## 291

*Success is the result of skills, not brilliance.*

## 292

*No one is better qualified to solve*

*your problems than you.*

## 293

*Entrepreneur: architect of personal dreams.*

## 294

*Excellence is a state of mind.*

## 295

*Research everything – observe everything
- analyze everything – test everything.*

## 296

*Good feedback is as precious as gold.*

## 297

*Big successes are the result of small changes.*

## 298

*Successful entrepreneurs predict the unpredictable and think the unthinkable.*

## 299

*Less is more, especially when you're a management consultant.*

## 300

*You can outdo anybody as long as your budget is big enough.*

## 301

*Ambition: dream with a deadline.*

## 302

*Take IT easy.*

## 303

*Exploit your competitor's weakness by exposing his greatest strength.*

## 304

*Insight is good, foresight is better.*

# 305

*Correlation is not causation!*

# 306

*Relativism is morally blind.*

# 307

*The biggest risk is not taking risks.*

# 308

*Be consistent, even when you're inconsistent.*

## 309

*Consultant: echo of a manager.*

## 310

*It's often wise to say nothing during a meeting.*

## 311

*Becoming a CEO is more pleasant*
*than being a CEO.*

## 312

*Leadership can't be taught, but it can be learned.*

## 313

*The only way we achieve high performance
is through the work of others.*

## 314

*Failure is a great teacher, but best met early in life.*

## 315

*One mentor is one more than most people get.*

## 316

*Escape natural selection by doing
the evolving yourself.*

## 317

*A good consultant gives a client a
bumpy and uncomfortable ride.*

## 318

*You can't grow long-term if you
can't eat short-term.*

## 319

*Success is not gained by perfecting the
known, but by seizing the unknown.*

## 320

*Being successful is about survival of the
'fitting', not survival of the 'fittest'.*

## 321

*Things change, so change things!*

## 322

*The best way to build a business buzz is to whisper.*

## 323

*Strive for unity without uniformity.*

## 324

*Consult a fool regularly.*

## 325

*The secret of success is to go strictly your own way.*

---

## 326

*Put respect on the business menu.*

---

## 327

*Good presentations do not equal good communication.*

---

## 328

*Anything you do repeatedly will get you 'there'.*

## 329

*As long as it's fun, don't worry.*

## 330

*Respect gives you a license to tell the truth.*

## 331

*Will is the greatest of all power multipliers.*

## 332

*Make more by doing less.*

## 333

*A solution is not an art project.*

## 334

*Simply being ambitious is not a strategy.*

## 335

*Expect less – pay more!*

## 336

*The question isn't whether you will survive, but how you will evolve.*

## 337

*It's not an experiment if you
know it's going to work.*

## 338

*The people who will benefit most from a
new technology are the last to adopt it.*

## 339

*You not only have to win; you
have to win your way.*

## 340

*Influence rushes in when you invite it.*

## 341

*Freedom multiplies the number of decisions you need to make.*

## 342

*Keep your eye not just on the headlines but also the trendlines.*

## 343

*Selecting is subtracting.*

## 344

*Create meaning out of uncertainty.*

## 345

*There is a rate of growth at which everybody fails.*

## 346

*Without information, a great
idea is only a short story.*

## 347

*Meeting: diarrhea of words.*

## 348

*Clarity: a manager's jewel.*

## 349

*Constraints drive innovation.*

## 350

*Personal Assistant (PA): manager of a manager.*

## 351

*Telling a story is more effective
than agonizing over rigor.*

## 352

*Leadership is not a gift but really hard work.*

## 353

*Climbing mountains is good, but*
*reaching summits is better.*

## 354

*Reputation is built on repetition.*

## 355

*Opportunity always starts with a relationship.*

## 356

*There is no security without performance, and*
*there is no performance without security.*

## 357

*A market is where someone's waiting for you.*

## 358

*Leadership is the silence between the words.*

## 359

*Never miss the significance of a new rival.*

## 360

*Synergies do not equal redundancies.*

## 361

*Best practices don't always travel well.*

## 362

*To lead is to choose.*

## 363

*The best price is a surprise.*

## 364

*Satisfied customers are not loyal.*

## 365

*Value equals benefits minus price.*

## 366

*You can't be normal and expect magnificent results.*

## 367

*Vision is only the start.*

## 368

*All good advice sings the same song.*

## 369

*While a single leader is often required, a collective leadership style is often more effective.*

## 370

*Consultants need to communicate empathy – not sympathy – for clients.*

## 371

*Judgment isn't luck.*

## 372

*Reputation will not get the deal done.*

## 373

*If you can't do a thing better than how it is already done, why do it?*

## 374

*The more important the task, the smaller the team needed.*

## 375

*The right comment is 'no comment'.*

## 376

*Does it really matter?*

## 377

*An advisor's responsibility is supplementing,
rather than supplanting, management.*

## 378

*Simple solutions are easier to understand.*

## 379

*A great leader transforms the will
to win into the will to serve.*

## 380

*Team player = trust builder.*

## 381

*Never overlearn the methodology
and underlearn the judgment.*

## 382

*Make excellent mistakes.*

## 383

*There is no safe way to have an idea.*

## 384

*Prestige: vessel for meaning.*

## 385

*Every executive decision is more about the executive than the decision.*

## 386

*You can only improve the ones who are already good.*

## 387

*The role of leadership is to anticipate the future before it happens.*

## 388

*No matter how good you are at something, there's always somebody better.*

## 389

*Give up a customer – do not compromise.*

## 390

*If at any point in time you say "we're good enough", that's the day you'll never be good enough again.*

## 391

*Reconsider is an option for an entrepreneur or manager, not for an advisor.*

## 392

*You haven't made a great decision until you've found a way to implement it.*

## 393

*Know when you know enough.*

## 394

*Failure = SUM (challenging management, change management, changing management).*

## 395

*The Holy Trinity: three arguments.*

## 396

*Reliability is the single most important dimension of quality.*

## 397

*Business is about understanding human nature.*

## 398

*A well-written report sings.*

## 399

*A great concept takes care of itself.*

## 400

*Depersonalize!*

## 401

*The best thing about new clients is that they come one at a time.*

## 402

*Reasonable people differ.*

## 403

*Exercising authority is a corruption of the skill-category concept.*

## 404

*Teamwork is not a dimension but the foundation of your work.*

## 405

*Your work should be better than your customer expects, yet not more than the situation calls for.*

## 406

*Loyalty is everyone's responsibility.*

## 407

*Good advisors are practitioners, not preachers.*

## 408

*To 'fit in' stop trying to fit in!*

## 409

*Corporations are less successful in people development than in customer development.*

## 410

*All problems have solutions and all solutions have problems.*

## 411

*The web never forgets.*

## 412

*The best way to get a good strategy is to develop a variety of strategies.*

## 413

*A person without information cannot take responsibility; a person who is given information cannot help but take responsibility.*

## 414

*You don't make money when you sell things; you make money when you help people make decisions.*

## 415

*Fail quickly so you can try again.*

## 416

*It is easier to advise from the back when you also get a chance to lead from the front.*

## 417

*Hot products are cool.*

## 418

*No organization is sounder than its judgments.*

## 419

*Budget approval meeting: play-off game.*

## 420

*Say it, don't present it.*

## 421

*Disruptive disease: toxic sameness.*

## 422

*Customers expect you to be good, but they also expect you to be even better tomorrow.*

## 423

*A writing problem is often symptomatic of a thinking problem.*

## 424

*If you make your expectations clear you will get exactly what you've specified 99 percent of the time.*

## 425

*People development is like motherhood*
*– everybody has a different theory.*

## 426

*It's much more difficult to copy the 'how to*
*compete' than the 'where to compete'.*

## 427

*Twitter account: post-modern business card.*

## 428

*Limit assessments to probabilities.*

## 429

*Your colleagues have the right to leave the meeting on schedule.*

## 430

*Treat every talk as though it were to be delivered on national television.*

## 431

*Satisfaction and overload are in the same category.*

## 432

*Make certain there is a clear quid pro quo.*

## 433

*We become what we measure.*

## 434

*The secret to competitiveness: competition.*

## 435

*Fall back on tradition and you may never get up.*

## 436

*Aim for the high-hanging fruit.*

## 437

*Find the window.*

## 438

*Firms must move from a one-culture organization to a one-organization culture.*

## 439

*When outcomes are not dominant over processes, measurement loses meaning.*

## 440

*Executives need to be mindlessly global and hopelessly local.*

## 441

*Premium is not luxury.*

## 442

*The essence of leadership: telling
the signal from the noise.*

## 443

*If you don't want a competitor
to buy it, don't sell it.*

## 444

*A revolution has to become a renaissance.*

## 445

*Magic is 'cool' but hard to replicate.*

## 446

*A reputation is only as good as*
*the clients it attracts.*

## 447

*Being known does not mean being loved.*

## 448

*Products fulfill needs, but experiences fulfill desires.*

## 449

*Consulting is more than giving advice.*

## 450

*Don't act, just be!*

## 451

*Vagueness leaves room for other people to fill in the details.*

## 452

*Don't let any system go unchanged for more than two years, or it will become too routinized.*

## 453

*If you can't implement, what good is a great plan?*

## 454

*Good ethics lead to great profits.*

## 455

*In the end everyone burns out.*

## 456

*Most people can stand adversity; very few people can stand success.*

## 457

*Passions never have to become professions.*

## 458

*Leadership in a vacuum has no impact.*

## 459

*Keep problems where they are least important and most manageable.*

## 460

*Never make excuses – make sacrifices!*

## 461

*What matters is not what you are,*
*but what you want to be.*

## 462

*Don't express, impress!*

## 463

*Don't substitute data for insight: data are*
*about the past, insight is about the future.*

## 464

*Manager: actor in his/her own play.*

## 465

*The best business plans are
written by market forces.*

## 466

*Competition is like warfare: easy
to start but difficult to end.*

## 467

*Entrepreneurs who like to eat fish
have to deal with big waves.*

## 468

*Asking is influencing.*

## 469

*There is one form of communication that
is always understood: the smile.*

## 470

*Image: fame on steroids.*

## 471

*If employees are not loyal to the organization,
customers won't be loyal either.*

## 472

*Learning should always happen
as a natural activity.*

## 473

*Tell them, tell them again, and then tell them again.*

## 474

*Differences in perception give rise to opportunities.*

## 475

*Value the value of values.*

## 476

*Precision promotes transparency.*

## 477

*Strategy implementation is not the consequence of strategy formulation, but the starting point.*

## 478

*Managers will compete harder for their own interests than for their company.*

## 479

*The first method for estimating the effectiveness of a manager is to look at the people around him.*

## 480

*The secret of success is constancy of impact.*

## 481

*The eight Rs of prosperity + progress:*
*Rethink, Redefine, Reuse, Reduce,*
*Renew, Redesign, Revisit, Recycle.*

## 482

*There isn't a company that is not*
*ripe for a few improvements.*

## 483

*Research or 'big data' is no substitute for thought.*

## 484

*Challenge: price of progress.*

## 485

*Purpose is the great lever of all things.*

## 486

*Nothing more enhances authority
than competitiveness.*

## 487

*Small opportunities are the
beginning of great empires.*

## 488

*The more global we become, the more local we act.*

## 489

*Convince through conviction or confusion.*

## 490

*The first quality of a great entrepreneur? – a 'cool' head.*

## 491

*It's better to act too quickly than it is to wait too long.*

## 492

*If everyone likes your work, it is probably not very interesting.*

## 493

*The only thing one never regrets*
*are loyal employees.*

## 494

*Do not compete too long with one competitor,*
*or you will teach him all your tricks.*

## 495

*Good management cures; good leadership cares.*

## 496

*The only thing between you and greatness is you.*

## 497

*It's not the facts that cause people to change: it's their opinions and perceptions about the facts.*

## 498

*The best definition of risk: when someone cannot pay.*

## 499

*Plans don't have meaning because they don't affect lives – actions do.*

## 500

*Stock your office coffee machine and fill the water cooler – on time, all the time.*

# 3 ABOUT THE AUTHOR

PIETER KLAAS JAGERSMA is a Dutch entrepreneur and leading authority on management and business strategy. He received a master of science degree in economics (summa cum laude) from Groningen University and a Ph.D. in economics from Tilburg University.

Pieter Klaas Jagersma is the founder of RONIN Investments, a research and investment firm. He joined Nyenrode Business University in the mid-1990s, and became the youngest business administration professor in Dutch history. He is also a (visiting) professor at other universities and business schools. His writings have been widely published. He is the author of 26 books and over 300 articles (for an overview see: www.jrcinternational.eu).

Pieter Klaas Jagersma serves on the supervisory and advisory boards of an array of international companies. He also serves as a counselor to the Dutch government. Earlier in his career, he worked at McKinsey & Company and as managing director of KPN Finance. He can be reached at pkj@wxs.nl

www.ingramcontent.com/pod-product-compliance
Lightning Source LLC
Chambersburg PA
CBHW072313210326
41519CB00057B/4896